Howdy

LIL' AMIGO

This book
belongs to: _____

From: _____

For my little Grayson,
and all the other super cool
little humans out there.
Always embrace your weird
and keep your cool.

AUSTIN IS COOL

AND ALSO TOTALLY WEIRD

STAY COOL

THE COOLEST THING ABOUT AUSTIN
IS THAT ANYTHING GOES,

SO JUST BE YOU, AND GET OUT THERE
AND DO SOME COOL THINGS.

AND GET BATTY
AT THE CONGRESS
AVENUE BRIDGE.

FOR SOME
LOCAL ODDITIES.

HISSSss

HEAR A COOL BAND

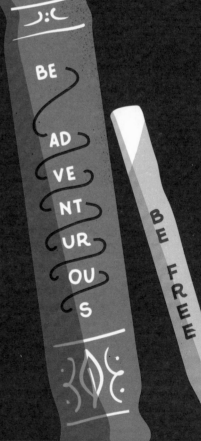

TIP YOUR HAT TO A
LOCAL LEGEND.

AND LEAVE YOUR MARK AT
THE HOPE OUTDOOR GALLERY.

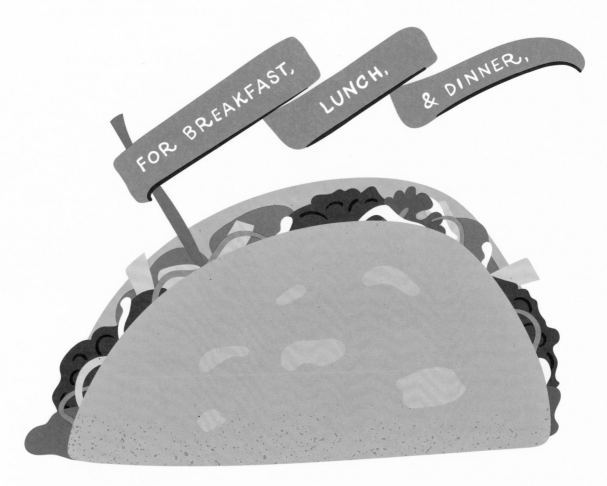

AND REVEL IN THE
GUACAMOLE!

GO WITH THE FLOW AT LADY BIRD LAKE

OR FIND A HOLE AND SWIM IN IT,
FOR A FRESH TAKE.

AND DO YOGA WITH A GOAT
ON YOUR BA-DON-KA-DONK.

EAT A BURRITO THAT'S AS BIG AS YO' FACE.

THEN TAKE A SIESTA
AT ZILKER PARK,

AND DIVE INTO THE
COOLEST SPOT IN TOWN
—BARTON SPRINGS POOL.

VISIT A LOCAL FARMERS' MARKET.

AND GET A FEAST FOR YOUR EYES

OR GO TO A FESTIVAL

WHERE ANYTHING FLIES.

BE A WILDFLOWER,

AND GET
A FRESH
PERSPECTIVE AT
THE PENNYBACKER
BRIDGE,

ON A
MOUNT BONNELL
RIDGE.

AND GET YOURSELF IN LINE
FOR SOME OF THE
TASTIEST BBQ YOU CAN FIND.

MEET EBERLY

the GREEN BELT

ZILKER

BEST

HILL Country

Rainey

Amy's

6th

ACL MUSIC FEST

JuiceLand

South LAMAR

DON'T LOSE
YOUR TWANG.
YETI
LOVE
KEEP IT LOCAL
DOG DAD
VIVA Leslie
SKATE OR DIE
Zilker OR BUST

KEEP IT WEIRD

y'all

Austin Is Cool, and Also Totally Weird
First Edition — June, 2022
Proudly Designed in Austin & Printed in Texas
on Eco-friendly Sustainable Paper
Copyright ©2022 MAYF Studio
ISBN 13: 978-0-578-54535-6

This book is a work of fiction, and is an interpretation of the Author/Illustrator's
perspective. It humbly references some of the coolest local Austin buildings, roads, brands,
musicians, artists, folks, sport teams, businesses, galleries, artwork, and local quirks,
but that does not constitute or imply their endorsement, recommendation or approval.

SXSW® is a registered trademark owned by SXSW, LLC

ACL® is a registered trademark of ACL Music Festival

Willie Nelson® is the man, the myth, the legend.

The "Willie for President" mural, is an original artwork
by Jacqui Oakley, Erick Montes & Joe Swec at
STAG Provisions on South Congress Avenue

"CAW", is an original artwork by Christian Moeller
at the Austin Central Library, downtown

The Angelina Eberly statue, is an original artwork
by Pat Oliphant on Congress Avenue

The Stevie Ray Vaughan Memorial, is an original
artwork by Ralph Helmick at Auditorium Shores

AUSTIN IS COOL.COM

THIS LITTLE BOOK INCLUDES A CAREFULLY
CURATED MIX OF COOLNESS, THANKS TO SOME
OF AUSTIN'S FINEST AND WEIRDEST:

Texas State Capital
Congress Avenue Bridge
Hotel San José
South Congress Avenue
Austin Central Library
STAG Provisions
HOPE Outdoor Gallery
Lady Bird Lake
Broken Spoke
Chuy's Tex-Mex
Hey Cupcake!
Austin City Lemons
Burro Cheese Kitchen

Zilker Metropolitan Park
Barton Springs Pool
Texas Farmers' Market at Mueller
SXSW Conference and Festivals
Pennybacker Bridge
Mount Bonnell
Franklin Barbecue
YETI
JuiceLand
Amy's Ice Creams
Long Center for the Performing Arts
Austin City Limits Festival
Austin Motel

THANKS FOR KEEPING
the SOUL of
AUSTIN ALIVE

See you
out there!

Author and Illustrator, Annie Mayfield, is a native Texan
with roots in really far West Texas. She has hung her hat in Austin
for over two decades, and is crazy-in-love with all of its quirks.
For the past 18 years, she has worked with clients both big and small
to tell their stories and build their brands. She's combined her love
of Austin, and storytelling in this canny little book
for all the cool kids out there.

After many days of exploring Austin together, this book was
dreamt up entirely during her son Grayson's nap time.
Weirdly enough, kiddos open your eyes to so many new things.
They're fearless explorers with vastly open minds, carefree spirits,
contagiously friendly smiles, and imagination for days; and they're
such an inspiration. Just like this book, you cool kids,
and Austin are what dreams are made of.

Mayf Dream Big!

THIS BOOK IS DEDICATED
TO THE ONES I LOVE. — AM

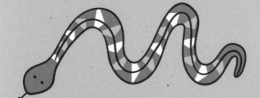